SUPER SISTERS

Super Sisters

Darren Deegan

Wren and Jaina are the best of friends, always playing games and running around together.

Jaina throws the ball to Wren, but she misses and it boops Wren on the nose. They both laugh.

Suddenly a call comes in on the Super Radio.

"Hello, who's there" asks Wren.

"It's Lucy, I need your help!" Says a squeaky voice over the radio.

"I came to watch the Dinosaurs marching south for the winter, but I fell and my foot is stuck between two rocks. The Dinosaurs will pass right through here any minute." Lucy says.

"Don't worry Lucy, Super Sisters are on the way," shouts Jaina.

The sisters arrive and see Lucy way across the field, right between two large rocks.

"She must have been climbing those rocks to get to a safe spot to watch the dinosaurs." Says Jaina.

"And now she's stuck! The dinosaurs are already marching in, what will we do?" Asks Wren
The girls put their heads together and think of a plan.

"I've got it!" Yells Jaina. "You can use the Super Helicopter to fly over there and move those big rocks with the claw."

"Brilliant idea," says Wren.

Wren runs back to the Super Helicopter and flies off across the field to save Lucy.

The Super Helicopter zooms across the field into position above Lucy.

"Don't worry Lucy, I'll have you out of there in just a minute." Wren cries from the cockpit of the helicopter.

Wren hits the winch button, lowering the cable and claw. The claw clamps onto the smallest rock. Wren hits the winch button again to pull the rock up and release Lucy's foot.

Lucy hears a loud snap and sees the winch cable break.

"Oh no, I'll never get out of here now!" Lucy cries.

Jaina watches the rescue from across the field and sees the cable break.

"Oh no, Wren won't have time to fix that cable."

Just then, she sees the Dinosaurs marching across the field from the other side.

"They're going straight towards Lucy!"

Jaina uses her super speed to run across the field in just a few seconds.

"I'm here Lucy, don't worry, we'll get you out of there."

She tries to move the rock, but it's just too heavy.

"There's no time, the Dinosaurs are here," Says Lucy

"Oh wait, I have an idea." Jaina says.

Just as the Dinosaurs reach them, Jaina uses her super scream!

The Dinosaurs have never heard anything like that before, and they run around Jaina and Lucy to get away from it.

"That was a close one," says Lucy, when the Dinosaurs have all passed by.

Everyone made it back to Super Hero Tower safely. The girls offered Lucy some juice, but they forgot robots don't drink! "Lucy, you were so brave out there." Says Jaina.

"Thanks, I just really wanted to see the Dinosaur march, I'm not a brave hero like you guys."

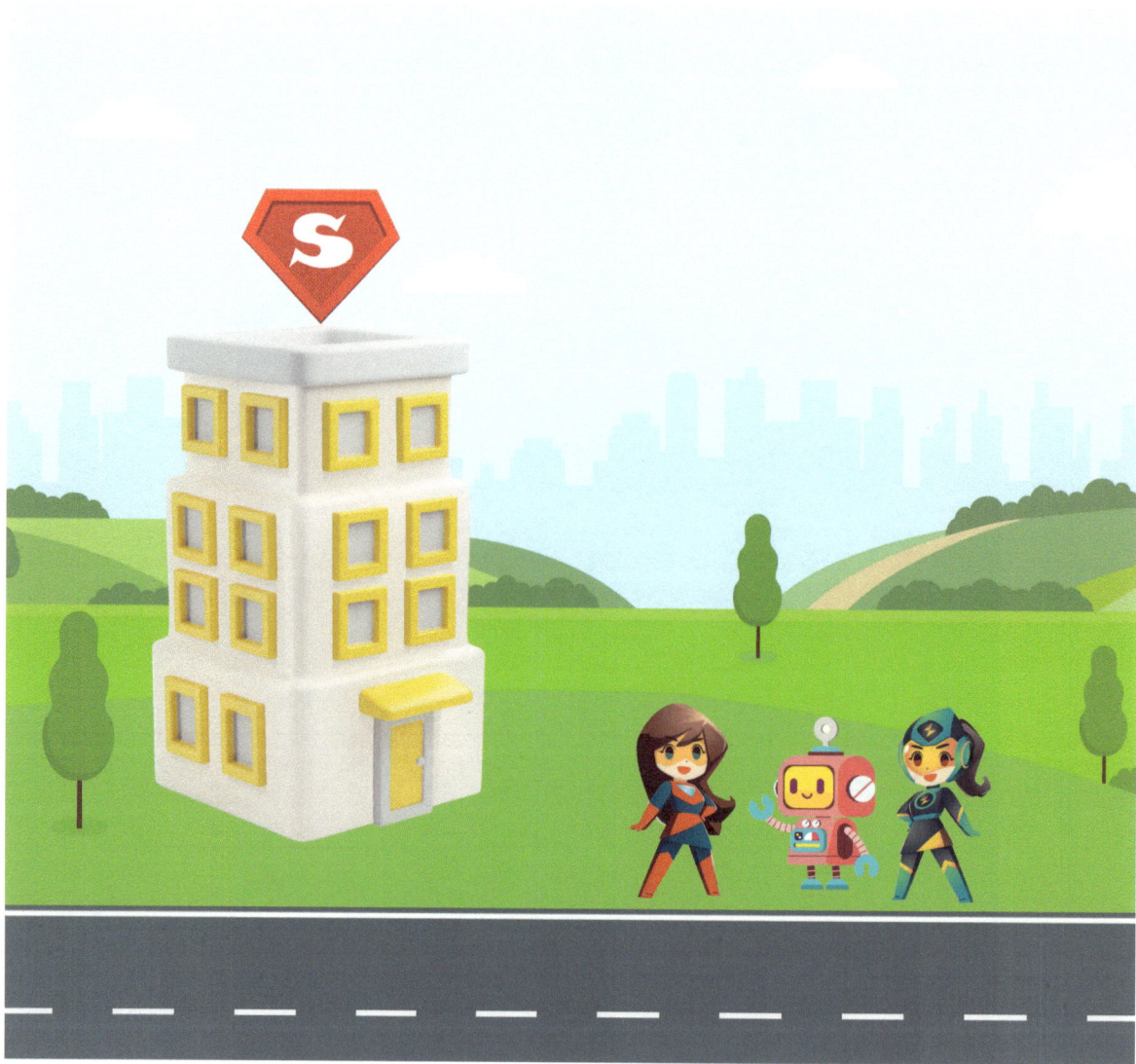

"You could be." Wren says, turning to Jaina. "Lucy should come join us, she could be a hero too."

"That's a great idea. What do you think Lucy?" Jaina asks.

Lucy looks so excited, "I'd love to."

Lucy joins the Super Sisters! She can't wait for fun adventures helping everyone.

www.ingramcontent.com/pod-product-compliance
Ingram Content Group UK Ltd.
Pitfield, Milton Keynes, MK11 3LW, UK
UKHW051014200125
453796UK00007B/36